From Seed to Sprout

A COLLECTION OF RAW THOUGHTS

KIJLEE GOODRICH

WESTBOW
PRESS®
A DIVISION OF THOMAS NELSON
& ZONDERVAN

WestBow Press books may be ordered through booksellers or by contacting:

WestBow Press
A Division of Thomas Nelson & Zondervan
1663 Liberty Drive
Bloomington, IN 47403
www.westbowpress.com
1 (866) 928-1240

ISBN: 978-1-9736-6237-2 (sc)
ISBN: 978-1-9736-6239-6 (hc)
ISBN: 978-1-9736-6238-9 (e)

Library of Congress Control Number: 2019907083

Print information available on the last page.

WestBow Press rev. date: 8/15/2019

Contents

Dedicated to my family.

Family: anyone or thing that has touched my life.

Thank you for teaching me:
To love all, no matter the differences.
To work for everything that you have.
To always help those when they are down,
Even when that means you give something up.
To know the difference of helping and hindering.
That you can be your greatest supporter or your worst enemy.
Most importantly, teaching me about God.

Thank you for your everlasting kindness and love.

Introduction

In my daily life, I try to take time to recognize beauty. The smell of fresh cut grass, the feeling of wet earth, the view of the sky in dawn or dusk, or the sound of music. A place in time where I allow my mind to relax, and allow my senses to be worked. To imagine there are greater things in this world to focus on rather than our itinerary or stresses. That there's more life and purpose than what we see or hear daily. That humanity is not what makes up this world, but that we are the keepers of it.

I constantly ask myself: how am I making this world better? How am I making the people around me better? How am I making myself better? That's what this book is the beginning of. Me telling my journey, my thoughts, my needs, or desires with the hope that it may impact another person. Where maybe we can start to learn who we are, why we are, and what we can do. I haven't lived an easy life, but who has? This is my growth through my exposition; there's so much more to live for and discover.

I also believe this world has lost sight of God and believing in something greater than ourselves or materialistic things. In that ignorance, we have been destroying humanity and our environment. Presently, there are many wars being fought that are affecting us now and that will dramatically change the future. I want to live in a world where I experience love daily. Where mental and physical health is not ignored or drugged. Where our environment is preserved and well-kept. Where there is equality for all genders, races, and ranks of society. A world where generations have a future.

Let us learn from the past, live peacefully in the present, and create a sustainable future. Let us push ourselves to believe again. To believe in humankind and our interactions with all living things. Let us realize what state the world is in before it's too late. Let us not neglect our responsibilities to our ancestors, ourselves, our children, and the organisms that don't have a choice.

You are the one that can change something in this world. You just have to decide if you'll do it or not. The choice is yours, just like every other human being.

Preface

For six years I have tried narrowing down a career choice. I worked on a farm, in two hospitals, and now for my county. I was interested in learning about everything, and I couldn't pinpoint one career that made me completely content. My family seemed baffled and amused by my continuous change in jobs, but it was frustrating for me. I knew I was meant to do more, and I knew I was meant to be more.

Writing has always been enjoyable for me. Something I did for fun, and something others enjoyed reading. I never really thought of it as a talent or a career choice. It wasn't until this past summer (2018) that my eyes were opened to the idea.

I had just recently been devoting myself back to God and spending my Sunday mornings at church again. My church was going over the book *Poverty, Riches and Wealth: Moving from a Life of Lack Into True Kingdom Abundance,* by Kris Vallotton. We had discussed wanting more as a congregation, and in our own individual lives. We decided to fast for two weeks. The first week we gave up something of our own choice. I chose all social media, I had such a habit of checking apps in the morning when I first woke that I had to delete them off my phone for the time being. The second week we fasted, we were to only eat one meal a day (different circumstances if you had medical conditions). Throughout the process, I found I had more time to write. I began spending at least two hours a day dedicated to it—when I would have otherwise been on social media. I realized that writing was my passion. I had been ignorant to it my whole life, and when I really thought about it, I felt so dumbfounded I hadn't realized it before. I also spent time reading the bible and speaking with the Lord.

I was amazed at what he revealed to me during those two weeks; business ideas, book ideas, and a picture of what my life could look like if I trusted Him and followed His direction. By the end of it, I knew I needed to publish a book. It was to be something that would allow an open door for more. So this is it. This is the first book. My exposition and journey of following God again. I hope you enjoy this, and find Him through it. Anything is possible with Him—you just have to be open to the idea.

My Mission

There was a day I was born.
That day,
I survived death.
That day,
I was given purpose:
Preserve life.

In the darkest of moments, there is chaos.
I have chosen to be clarity,
To show there is nothing to fear from
darkness but rather learn from it—
To know its weaknesses,
To know its every move,
To know how to defeat it.

I have chosen to speak and write truth,
To help preserve the world around us and the
souls of others who walk this earth,
To promote love and selflessness,
To change the standard quality of today,
To push for more—
Which might be less—
To stop destruction.

The hope, belief, and knowing that
words hold imaginable power,
The Bible, declarations, and names—
They hold history and keys to our future generations,
Never forgotten once read or heard.

In the middle of it all,
I will stand among the brave,
Embracing the freedom to live a better life—
To not survive, but fully live.

The preservation of life should be locked in
a seed and planted among our hearts,
Blossoming with a new mind, heart, and helpful hands.
That is my mission:
To write the seed,
To share the seed,
To plant the seed,
To preserve life,
To preserve the old—new today.

Remember

I'm not telling people how to live their lives;
I'm telling people how I'm going to live mine.
These are
my thoughts,
my opinions,
my memories,
my wants,
and the things God has shown me.

These are my truths.
I will not ignore them.

3

Radicle—The Start
Stage 1

Birth of a Nation

Blood-soaked soil forever embedded under the nails
Screams, and faces forever seen and
heard with the shut of an eye—
Some generations forever lost,
Some generations forever found.
Many perished and became the foundation of this country.
Their pain, passion, and sacrifice must never be forgotten.
Their fight for freedom, peace, and
righteousness must burn within us still.
Let our voices be heard when it is time to speak.
Let our ears be open when it is time to listen.
Let this country become wise once more,
and fight for the one true thing—
God.

The Hand of Peace

Music is the language of our souls,
Connecting all decades, ages, genders, races, cultures, and
events at any point in time,
Past, present, future.
Music gives connection.
It gives no loneliness.
It gives only love.

Dementia

Old faces,
Wrinkled hands,
Gentle hearts,
Shattered minds,
Loss and discovery.
Fear,
Hopelessness,
Loneliness,
Creative
Entrapment,
Limitless views.
Warriors
In need of love,
In need of awareness,
Abandoned by humanity,
Comforted only by God—
Still His children,
Never forgotten,
Renewed in heaven.

Timepiece

Time is important.
On a clock,
It never changes.
It's always steady.

In our lives,
Time is different.
It's linked to our minds and emotions,
Where the clock doesn't matter.
The speed of time changes constantly.

In the end,
We will notice
How fast it really passes
And how it will continue on without us.

A Tune of Voice

A rhythm,
A beat to a chord,
A soft whisper of wind.

There is little noticed in voice,
Yet so much control it possesses.

Thoughtless minds brought back to memories once heard,
Changing their whole existence.

Fragments of moments stored forever,
All revisited with one voice,
One person,
One feeling.

A song,
A word,
A vow.

It all means nothing until spoken by the right person.
With the right voice,
With the right feeling.

Voice releases power, belief, and trust.
You can feel the good or the evil.
You can believe the good or the evil.
A voice can be a spell of entrapment
Or a declaration of freedom.

A voice is what we need.
We need to hear others.
But in a crowd we need to recognize our own.
We need to be comfortable with our sound
And how it can affect others.

A drum is played,
A string strung,
A gentle touch on wind chimes.
My voice has been heard.

Worship

Movement,
Dance,
Power.
Words that change mood.
Words that change everything.
Whispers from instrumental notes.
Praise,
A bridge from earth to God.
Every nation,
Every culture,
One language.
One art.
A presence.
A place of being whole,
Where no time passes.
Expectance,
Acknowledgment of royalty.
Honor,
Pleasure,
Peace.
Freedom to be ourselves.
Freedom to be more.
How Great Is Our God.

Lake Michigan

White cotton clouds
Observing in the sky,
Releasing wind into the air.

Smiles, laughter.
Sun shining so bright
Upon little faces and little hands.

Grandparents sit between two trees,
Observing in white plastic chairs,
Whispering about their young blood.

Sparkling water, dancing waves,
Warmth and chill in a twist.
Children play,
Wishing to be mermaids and fish.

Small suits, tan skin—
Young love.

A destination of all happiness,
All thoughts, all ages.

A destination of paradise.

Black-Eyed Susan

When I woke,
She was there to love.
Her golden petals reached to the ground to comfort me.
She was soft, beautiful, and different—
Wild,
Vibrant,
And classic.
She taught me her ways and His.
She was there when my heart began to feel.
She was there when my mind turned.
Through hurt, pain, and rebellion, she still loved.
I give Him my thanks for allowing such a person,
Inspiration,
And faith to overcome my life.
Could there be that many love stories embedded in one flower?
Yes.
My black-eyed Susan,
My grandma,
My beginning.

Her Color is Yellow

She is wild,
She is free,
Galloping from the past,
Not afraid to survive
For she had endured much.
Her mane long,
Muscles strong,
Color painted and unique.
Fire burning within her eyes.
She was not broken until she was alone.
She was full of love,
Wanting a friend.
Yet some feared.
Only the fearless gained her respect as she knew their hearts.
A wild spirit cannot be tamed.
It will always be unpredictable
For it has yet to tame itself.

The Giver

A small gift of friendship.
A small gift of love.
A small gift of comfort.

A hand to hold.
An ear to listen.
A tongue to speak.

The greatest gifts in life show people they're not alone
And that they never will be.

It gives hope.
It gives happiness.
It gives life.

Parents either create or demolish minds full of dreams.

The Creation of Two

When I look in the mirror, I see you both.
I see your colors and features.
I see your tears and smiles.
I see your love and pain.
I see my past—
My childhood.

Molded From Fire and Ice

A child made from innocence,
A child made from immaturity,
A child made from freedom,
A child made from love,
A child made between the moon and the sun.
A child that changed it all for them.
The child who became their earth.

Climate Change

The moon and the sun loved like none other,
Kissing when they had seconds,
Dancing between the days and nights.
But their love was short,
Burned by the distance,
Crushed by the differences.
The greatest love story,
The greatest tragedy.

Earth was never the same without them both.

We had each other when we had no one else.

To the Parent That Became Both

We grew together.
We learned together.
We felt together.
We survived hardships together.
Intertwined since birth,
Our lives will always search for each other.
For you are my friend, a companion, and my comforter—
The moon that comforts the stars,
And the sun that leads the days.

We cannot judge.
We are not God.

What is to Blame?

Dark,
Strong,
Bubbly;
What is it about you that has consumed so many lives?
You change minds.
You change hearts.
You soak into the flesh, toxifying cells.

But maybe it is not you.
Maybe it is the glass that holds you,
The glass that reflects the image of a soul.
The glass that plays our secrets in front of our eyes.

But maybe it is not the glass.
Maybe it is the owner of the eyes that seek the truth.
Maybe it's us and our own secrets.
Maybe we're the ones consuming so many
lives because we've consumed our own.

All I've ever wanted is to be loved.

22 Wishes and Counting

I'm still just a girl,
Wishing her father would learn to grow,
Wishing he would learn to put another thing before himself,
Wishing he would learn to forgive and move on,
Wishing he saw his own potential and the love in his heart,
Wishing he saw his story within my eyes and felt what I felt.
Maybe then he would know how much love I have for him.

Maybe next years added candle will be the
trick to making my wishes come true.

My Blood is Your Blood

I am hard on you because I look up to you.
I expect more of you because I see the
potential within your eyes and heart.
I see a part of me in you,
And I do not want myself to fail.
I need you to win,
So I know that I can win.

Try These On

If only you could see your beauty from my eyes,
maybe then you would learn to love yourself.

The Creator of Picasso and Mozart

God is the ultimate artist.
He created earth,
The space of ever-changing colors,
music, and moods by season.
Not one day is painted the same.
Not one day is conducted the same.
How is it that I get to be painted so uniquely?
How is it that He chose the colors to define me?
How is it that no other person will replicate my scenes?
Maestro, never stop the rainfall.
As You feel near.
Artist, never stop the uniqueness of color
As I see Your eye for beauty.
I cherish Your work and effort.
It is now ours to view,
A gallery for all to see,
A live performance for all to hear.

The Deed Said, "Share"

Dirt,
Rock,
Sand,
Grass:
They are all beneath our feet.

Moon,
Stars,
Sun,
Clouds:
They are all above our heads.

Beating hearts,
Open eyes,
Listening ears:
They are all in between.

We share all of this
With every person,
Every nation,
Every language,
Every skin tone,
Every religion,
Every creature,
Every generation.

We share the world.
We share our world.

We share the environment.
We share our environment.

We share the past, present, future.
We share our past, present, future.

We share a life.
We share our lives.
We share our earth's life.

Bleeding reminds us we're alive.
With bleeding comes pain.

Anger consumes.
Anger frightens.
Anger always ends with a problem.

Earth is the space between heaven and hell,
Where both are present.

Hypocotyl—The In Between
Stage 2

The Girl Inside the Writer

Her eyes were emerald green
With reflections of vast gardens.
Kindness was her strength,
Love her weakness.

She loved the smell of fresh-cut roses, lavender oil, and red wine.
She lived in a dream where reality was all she wanted it to be.
She wondered when she'd wake or when things would break.
She was young.
She was beautiful.

A heart of gold,
A mind full of curiosity
Awaiting adventure.
Days filled with self-failure,
Yet a smile on her face.

She wanted to crumble,
But she is strong.
She believed like a child
That humankind can and will be kind.
That God will provide.

She listened to the art of Debussy, Bob Dylan, Eminem, and Alice
in Chains.
She was in search for emotion, the feeling of fire, and connection.
The power of becoming full potential.

Modest and wild.
She loved running in empty fields of grass and climbing cliffs to
watch lake and ocean waves dance.
Different,
Lost in the eyes of others.
She was free and fearless.
She would lead.

A calling like Moses,
And the blood of nations—
Irish, Scottish, French, German, Native American.
America her home.

She's a fighter till the end, like her blood before her.
Surviving plagues and wars.
She is herself.
She is me.
A queen in training.

Her Fuel

She did not have a favorite type of music.
All that mattered was whether she felt the instruments or not.
There had to be movement in her soul.

Poet

We are people, artists, and musicians.
Kissing sheets of paper, leaving our marks on the world.
Notes, words, colors.
Speaking language from the soul,
Uncovering truth.
Purpose decided by God.
To change one, two, or three.
New discovery,
New creation.
Some understand,
Others feel.
Gifted since birth,
Gifted till death.
A drop of poet's blood.

First Sight of Snow

Flecks of white
Free falling.
Do they reach their arms to the sky?
Asking someone to grab them before they hit the ground?
Piling on one another.
Waiting to be trampled or melted away?

Or do they gracefully dance,
Knowing they only get one chance to be free and fly?
White, plain white,
A beautiful blank canvas.
Cold to the touch but beautiful sight.

Reminiscent Love

I was different when I was with you.
It was that feeling of being lost and
found all in the same moment.
And I was happy.

The Realm of Dreams

Dreams are the heart's desires.
Dreams are part of a world no one can explain.
Love and pain play their own game,
Telling tales of things to come,
Or implanting childish hopes of the perfect fantasy.
Good and evil both share their chills,
Which ride up the spine,
Caging lungs that release no air
For there may be a higher presence.
History, politics, and futuristic possibilities
Evoke fear, bravery, and discovery.
Ticking bombs, lost wars, epidemics,
Frantic thinking, or predictions.
Meaningless or truth.
A wormhole into a world no scientist can explain,
Or a place of imaginary existence that has no end.
Creating every thought we haven't thought,
Setting the stage for all files locked far away.
Paths we could take, people we could choose.
Adventures we want to have, fears that hold us in shackles.
The dream world is a world with no explanation.
No explanation at all.

First Love

Every touch, every look, every whisper.
They're all putting me under.
To forget what has happened will never be possible.
My mind and heart have changed.
I have changed.

I don't feel lost anymore.
I've found a connection that makes me
vulnerable yet invincible.
Moments like these don't feel human.
Love has to be God's gift to us all.
Love isn't weakness;
It is power.

As with all power, it can either build you up or break you down.

Only God knows the secrets we hold.

La Fin

Light, you are fading.
Colors, you are darkening.
World, you are being destroyed.
Dirt is no longer dirt.
Food is no longer food.
Humans are no longer humans.
We have been processed.
All eyes are on us.
Our strings are being pulled.
Our wages have been set.
The poor are poor.
The rich are rich.
The strong are strong.
The wise are wise.
There are those who play their parts.
There are those who watch the play.
And there are those who write their own scripts.

Grocery Store vs. Train Ride

Without any question,
We can trust a person we've never met with
the food that nourishes our bodies.
Yet we can't fully trust the person sitting next to us.

Chemistry

What is it that keeps us locked in fear?
Is it the reaction something might have?
Or is it the decision and words we have to choose?

Hopelessness and Knowing More

Days pass
As I look around,
I see and hear the same things I felt the day before.
Same faces,
Same conversations,
Same email checking,
Same rushing lunch,
Same tiredness,
Same waste.

As I lie in bed,
I stare at the fabric of the blanket.
I notice every detail.
Every fiber.
I stare at my hand;
I move my fingers as though it's the first
time I've discovered movement.
I'm exhausted yet afraid to fall asleep.
Fearing to wake up in tomorrow, twenty years forward,
To find myself in the same spot.

I need to feel.
To feel happiness,
To feel passion.

What have I done not to deserve it?
The sun is setting.
My eyelids are falling to the ground to rest.
Please tell me tomorrow will be different,
Tomorrow will be worth it.

Miracle Love

Water and sand always find each other.
When there is drought and we find each other,
We will then have our answer.

Then and Now

Tears build and break.
Memories playfully dance,
Projecting past times within the present.
What world do I live in?
Both.
One with outcomes that are familiar
and
One with outcomes that are still being decided.
Which do I like better?
Undecided.
One shows me what went wrong when I chose
and
One tells me to choose again.
Decisions, possibilities,
They change every moment.
They change every life.
I cannot change the past,
but
I can change the future
By what I do or say now.
I reflect on the past too many times;
I need all of me here.
A wave goodbye to things behind,
and
A wave hello to the things ahead.

There is never a time when change is impossible.
However, the longer the issue waits, the
harder the process will be.

Blue Bird

Her feathers were bright blue and perfectly kept.
Her eyes green, like the grass plains she had dreamt to see.
She viewed the world from her family's brown-colored bowl.

Would the wind carry her to her desires,
Or would gravity pull her to her death?

Would she fly among the brave, telling world tales,
Dancing among the clouds?

Or would she lie upon the dry sand she
had become familiar with?

She had to decide.
Live or die.

She jumped into the unknown,
Only knowing she had to try.

Balance

You can disappoint yourself.
You can be proud of yourself.
Acknowledge both.
Find balance in the middle.
Let that help guide you.

Catch and Release

Open your hands;
Release what you want to keep.
Watch the wings flap and fly away.

You will feel relieved.
You will feel weightless.
You will feel new.

Meditation is not a religion.
It is a process of finding peace within ourselves.

A Plant's Life

Planted in a field,
Michigan soil became my home.
I've seen darkness
And feared the things I cannot see
But feel and hear.
My Creator gave me strength.
Inch by inch I grew,
Pulling and pushing my way through.
When I finally touched the sky,
My arms embraced the beauty of daylight.
The sun cradled my face
And showed me the world.

It was not until I met the moon and stars that I realized
There was more to life than what was directly in front of me.
Would I ever grow tall enough to touch the stars?

My Creator trimmed,
Nourished,
And fed my needs.
As I grew old enough,
I thanked Him with fruit.
He trusted our relationship
And knew it was strong enough to produce something rare
And better than those before me.
Without testing,
He trusted,
And gave those whom He loved a piece of me.

In my old age,
I have learned to trust without fear, and
love all those my Creator loves.
In it all,
I have found purpose.
Without touching the stars, I had reached them.

Foliage—The New
Stage 3

Age of Discovery

Is it wrong for me to be courageous and follow my heart?
To follow a career that is completely me?
To be an artist where money doesn't
force my hands or my mind,
But to be led by my soul and my thoughts.
To be led by my feelings?
That is the happiness I want.
The happiness of feeling free.
To break the chains.
To see sunlight after being put in a box.
To feel the warmth after feeling the cold cement.
To view myself.
To know myself.
To set foot upon green grass and feel
the earth move underneath.
Surrounded by nature.
Surrounded by love.
Surrounded by God.

Stepping out of today into the garden of Eden.

The Six Year Pilgrimage

At a ski resort, I learned how to speak.
On a farm, I learned how to enjoy physical labor.
In a hospital kitchen, I learned pride and determination.
As a hospital nurse assistant, I learned to care about the souls
rather than the work.
As an administrative assistant, I learned to lead without fear
and found that I could do anything I learned.
As a writer, I found myself.

Let your passion be your career.
Let everyday be the new best day.

Note to Self

Look at you.
You're awake.
Get ready; you're going to conquer today.

Remember, you are important.
You will change this world.
You will not be judged based on gender, race,
age, money, or degree of education.
For you are so much more than all of that.

You have a purpose.
A journey.
A wonderful discovery for yourself and others.

Light this world with kindness.
Do not fear it.
Do not fear any of it.

Know you might run into obstacles.
Know not everyone will like you.
They will try to tear you down.
But as long as you love and trust yourself,
everything will be fine.

You are beautiful,
No matter what age.
You will bloom with the same color and beauty each season,
Surprising yourself with your courageous strength.

Tell the doubtful part of you no,
For doubt does not exist within faith.

You may grow tired.
You may begin to question.
But today is not that day.
Today is another day you begin to know yourself.
Today is another day they will know you.

Smile for the enemy is watching.
Smile for you are in this fight.

Protector, Comforter, Father

Though none go with me,
Alone in the kingdom, I will walk with You in hand.
Through the valley of bones and modern society norms,
We shall walk through the streets where
the impossible is possible.
Where evil lurks and the devil's whisper lingers in the air.
Where he hides his face in the shadows
and crevices of the night.
We shall walk past him, shining our light in his face,
Blinding him and his control.

We will not laugh in his face but shed a single tear
For all the minds he's controlled,
For all the lives he's ruined,
For all the dead he's claimed.

We will knock needles from arms;
Wipe white powder from noses;
Seal lids to vodka;
Stop the fighting between ourselves, others, and nations;
Soak the tears of innocent hearts;
Mend the fails of love.

You will touch souls and heal pains,
Teaching them Your ways and Your unending love.
Fear will be crushed, and people will be settled.
The strength You'll give will keep me and others walking.

You will protect for You do not send soldiers
into battle without sword and shield.

You will cover my eyes to what I need not see.
You will cover my ears to what I need not hear.
Change starts here.
It will then uncontrollably eat its way
through the city, state, and nation.
Nothing will stop it.

Though none go with me, I shall go with You.

Elevated Torch

I do not fear darkness.
I appreciate it.
It makes the light more clear to see.

God does not want us to fear
Or hide from things,
Issues,
Situations,
Addictions,
But rather recognize that they are there.

The same goes for darkness and light.
We must recognize both and decide where we stand.

The light will accept you.
It will show who you are:
Flaws,
Imperfections,
Rarity.

The darkness will hide you.
It may even hide you from yourself.
You can get lost in darkness with no vision or path to direct.

Eventually, you need to be able to venture into the dark,
In the end, becoming the light
In search of others who may have been lost on
the same path you were found dying on.

To live in light
Or die in darkness.
Only you can decide the hand you hold,
The path you take,
And how you choose to live.

Choices change everything.
No choice is still a choice.

SOS

All I've wanted is a diagnosis of the consistent
physical pain and feeling of being sick.
It wasn't that I wanted something to be wrong.
I just didn't want to be alone with it anymore.
I wanted help.
I wanted to know that it wasn't all in my head.

Maybe I didn't need a diagnosis.
Maybe I just needed to change my habits.

Why I've Chosen Him

He was there when no one else was.
His hand always stayed strong, ready to hold mine
Or pull me from my mess.

He walked with me, even when I chose to ignore His direction.
He listened even when I did what He warned against.
He still loved when I was angry and did not get my way.

He never left.
He never moved.
He never abandoned,
Even when I had abandoned Him.

How could something so great, so mighty,
so powerful love something like me?

That is love.
To love something that you yourself didn't think you could love.
Someone to love your words, actions, thoughts.
Someone who loves so great that your
hurts, pains, and sins disappear.

A friendship so great that love triumphs every time.
That is my God.
My Savior.
My King.
My friend.

The Star of Bethlehem

Imagine the raindrops that hit His face
Or the sand that lay beneath His feet.
The wind that brushed His hair
Or the stones that heard His voice.

The people who saw His grace have lived and gone.
But the earth still remembers Him;
The earth still remembers His story.

The night He was born,
The days He performed miracles,
The day He died,
The night He rose.

If only the earth could speak of His love and journey.
Maybe then we would see how foolish humanity has become
And be reminded of what we have forgotten.
Maybe then we would know
The star that was born one night in Bethlehem
Still lives on today.

Jesus became the star,
Igniting people's souls and creating a new light to be found in
His followers.

A King who was born wrapped in cloth, lying in straw,
Serenaded by angels,
Bowed to by all animals.

Let us remember,
Royalty is not defined on the outside but rather the star that
burns within.
Let us know,
Not all have forgotten Him.

Let us pray,
That we might hear those stories someday.
To feel what it was like to talk to the highest King.
To feel what it was like to listen to His voice.
To see the light within Him.

The birth of the King changed the world.
Let us celebrate, and be thankful for all that has happened
because of it.
Let us grow through His words and our God.
Let us learn how to burn brighter.

We bow to You.
Thank You for blessing us with this glorious day.
For it was the start of something greater.

We need to start wanting what we need
instead of wanting what we want.

2018

The current society is trying to erase our history.
It will never happen.
We have deeper understanding and cravings for knowledge.
We as humans will always wonder
Where we came from,
Who our ancestors were,
How the world affected them when they lived.
Why would we want to erase their lives?
Why would we want to disturb the past?
Let us learn from it, and give it peace.

Warning for the Present

We need to stop trying not to feel.
Realize this world needs more love.

The best thing we can do for ourselves
and others is to become selfless.
Boundaries are built, but it's not about us.
It's about the people surrounding our
lives and next generations.

We need to look at the past before history repeats itself again,
Or before we get to the point where
history just stops being written.

There is beauty in the past.
Do not shame it all.

All Weather Needed

Storms brew.
Black clouds surround.
Lightning strikes.

Fights break.
My thoughts circle.
Attacks are made.

Rain falls,
Soaking into the soil.

Tears fall,
Soaking into my heart.

Cold, gloomy days.

Cold, gloomy days.

Then the sun peaks out of the corner,
Shining warmth into the day.

Then he smiles out of the blue,
Sending warmth into my day.

A flower jumps out of the dirt,
Sending its petals into the air.

My legs begin to dance.
My arms embrace in a hug.

It was harder for me to handle his acceptance rather than his disappointment.

We'll truly see how much time was wasted
when we finally admit our own behavior.

My Other Half

Can love be so powerful that no circumstance can break it?
No fear,
No other power,
No choice.

I can't imagine life without him.
His eyes, his heartbeat, his voice.
They're all things I didn't expect to cherish.
But I do.
I look forward to being close to them everyday.

When I'm near him, I see our future.
Our children.
Our story and journey.

Time stops, and it's everything I've ever wanted.
Everything I've wished for.
Everything I've prayed for.

He has become my favorite human on earth.
My best friend.
My partner.
My lover.
Forever my husband.

There's nothing I'll ever forget
And something I'll always feel.
This is just the beginning,
The beginning to us.

My heart is a pantry full of memories
of you and fulfilled needs.
It will forever be storage for your love.

I Will Not Hide My Vulnerability

Music is my drug.
Sex is my stress release
Where my spirt is free with him.
Pen and paper are my thought release,
Where all of me is naked.
Being bare in a world where all see imperfections
Instead of admitting beauty and thanking truth.
But I still choose it.
And I would everyday.
To be in love every day with every day,
In hand with one man.
On a journey playing the best tunes,
And my thoughts leading the way.
God, that is my prayer:
To show people this imperfect life is beautiful,
To show embracing nakedness of the
mind and soul is beautiful.
My soul is raw, and it will always be Yours.
Why hide the truth when it is not wrong?
Why hide the truth when it is me?
Why hide the truth when it is a piece of You?

Amour

She soaks her body in lavender and patchouli oils.
Washes her hair with sage and coconut oil.
Cleanses her face with German naturals.
She braids her mane and walks barefoot on fresh soil, with ink
showing on her foot.
She stands for love—
The love for herself, the love of the earth, and the love of man.

One Shot of Roasted Daniel's

Black coffee is the morning's whiskey.
Bitter and burning,
With just enough strength to get you through a moment of
weakness.

Miracles happen when we surrender to the belief of faith.

My Dearest Daughter

There will be a day when you'll be able to decide,
To choose right from wrong,
To follow your head or your heart,
To stand alone or together,
To fight for your own beliefs or ignore them.

There will be a day when you will stand
on this earth and all evil will fear,
For your eyes will see truth,
Your ears will listen,
And your words will be spoken without fear.

This world is yours.
These flowers are yours to grow and lie in.
These stars are yours to gaze upon and reach for.
These mountains are yours to climb and dream from.
Everything you could ever wish for is in front of you.
Don't settle for less
For you are worthy of so much more.

I promise to help show you the world as it is and what it can be.
I promise to show you how to preserve
the goodness in our lives.
I promise to show you how to hope and
live on when you think you cannot.
I promise to comfort you when you need someone there.
I promise to watch you become the woman
you've always been able to be.
I promise to love you through it all.

Everyday is new.
Everyday there's a bit of old.
Everyday since you've come into existence,
you've started to change this world.
And there will be a day when you realize it.
A day when you know who you've been called to be.
A day when you become her.

I love you, my sweet little girl.
For always and forever.

My Little Prince

There will be a day your eyes will open, and
you'll see the color of the world.
There will be a day your legs will learn to walk,
and it will be hard to keep you near me.
There will be a day your words will make
sound, and it will be hard to answer you.

There will be a day when you notice thankfulness
and happiness in the littlest of things.
There will be a day when you notice cruelty
and realize you emit some of it.
There will be a day when you notice that
change in human behavior is needed.

There will be a day you'll turn into a
king and take on the kingdom.
It will be your responsibility to be a warrior in battle,
To trust your shield and sword,
To follow your head and heart,
To know right from wrong.
And the army will follow.

When questioned, you will answer.
When there is no path, you will see one.
When there is darkness, you will be a beacon.
At all times, you will lead.
At all times, you will listen.
At all times, you will love.

Never settle for less for you are worthy of so much more.
You will learn, you will fight, and you will lead.

Through it all, I will guide.
Through it all, I will comfort.
Through it all, I will love.

Always and forever.

There will be a day you will come into existence.
That day will be the start of a new beginning.

For All Women

You may not be my mother.
You may not be my sister.
You may not be my friend.
But I will embrace you.

If we subject ourselves to anger and revenge,
we will only become what we've hated.

Equal Importance In Every Role

Sons are just as important as daughters.
Husbands are just as important as wives.
Fathers are just as important as mothers.

Men are just as important as women.

Unity is the only way a war can be won.

Stitches

Forgiveness isn't easy.

It seals wounds
So we don't have to keep feeling the pain.
It helps us move onto happiness.

The scars remind us of what we've survived
And what we'll not allow ourselves to endure again.

Destined Love

On earth we stood.
Two different lands,
Yet the same air passing by.
I heard your sweet whispers.
I heard your gentle laugh.
How familiar it seemed.
How new it felt.
Years went by.
I searched high and low,
Climbing trees and mountains,
Diving in waters and tunnels.
After so much time,
It took one second.
In the middle of it all,
I found you.

Praise in Every Second

Yesterday I was thankful.
Today I am thankful.
Tomorrow I am blessed.

Believing without doubt or fear,
Knowing how big and great your God is,
Knowing that anything is possible with Him.
He hears prayers.
He sees our wants and desires.
But He knows our needs.
He provides for His children based on purpose.

He deserves trust.
He deserves credit.
He deserves praise.
Even when we only see part of the picture or plan.
We don't need to understand.
We don't need to know all the details.
We just need to be thankful in every given moment.

Miss Feline

Your eyes are gentle,
With a spark found in all innocent creatures—
A spark of life.

You are wild yet allow connection.
You trust.
You rely on me.

Knowledge in humans may have a different depth,
But why do we justify our actions when
treating an animal less than ourselves?
Are we not animals too?

They are themselves.
We are us.
And we all inhabit the same world.
Yet we are the ones who are destroying the entire
environment all creatures need to survive.

Maybe it's not about us.
Maybe it's about them,
The ones who can't live unless we let them.
The ones who don't have a voice.
The ones who don't have a choice.

My green-eyed cat
Showed me her world.
Apart from running through green grass, catching
butterflies, and dancing under blue skies,
It was simple:

Eat, sleep, and love as long as you can.

Before the instinct of survival kicks in,
Before the unpredictable instinct of humans kicks in,
Before we all become extinct.

Animal lives are short.
Why not make that time the best for them?
Which, in return, will make it the best
for our future generations.
Where we all might just live forever.

Decomposed

Days I see dead animals on the road, I wonder,

If those were humans,
Would someone then show sympathy for their lifeless bodies?
Would someone then give them a proper burial,
Shedding at least a single tear?
Would someone then show some kind of compassion for those
wild and free?
Maybe they would even find the people who took the lives,
The people who felt the shock,
Or the people who passed on their lifeless souls.

When we think to replace an animal with a human, does the
situation still seem justified?

The capability of goodness is within us all.

A Simple Wish for a Complex World

The wind whispers, telling secrets of the pines
While it dances across iced mountain tops.
Journeying across seas, grasslands, and cobblestone streets,
Settling down in a quiet town
Where freshwater ponds and lakes grew
to home many fish and humans.

The trees talk.
The trees listen.
And only the wind hears their thoughts.

The wind pushes colored leaves into tiny hands,
Granting little wishes of ponies or dreamed loves.
The wind itself wishes to grant preservation.

Preservation for its friends.

The streams of water.
The beds of fish.
The roots of new vegetation.
The nutrients in the soil.
The couple holding hands.
The family playing in the park.
The air it all consumes.

The wind would grant any child this wish,
But it had never been wished before.

Time went on, and the children grew.
They kept wishing but still not the very
wish they would truly need.

The streams dried up.
The fish were found no more.
The soil became dust.
No couples held hands.
Families were split.
The air began to escape.

The wind watched and heard no more from the trees.
The wind heard cries and prayers from the humans below.
If only they had listened to the pines' secrets,
They would have heard them say,

"We are dying because of you.
Please take care of us
So that you may take care of yourselves.
If you do not,
You will begin to die as well.
Please love us
For we love you."

If only they had wished for more with the simplest wish of all.

In a split second, it all could be gone.

Checkmate

Where there is fault, there is truth.
Where there is truth, there are honesty and bravery.
It takes courage to be a warrior.
It takes bravery to stand when all others cower
Or when things should be questioned.
It takes dedication and strength to be a leader.
But it takes discernment, wisdom, and humility to be a king.

Claim who you want to be.
Call it out.
Walk it out.
Believe fully and become full.

There is a battle brewing.
There are positions on a chessboard
God has called us to take up.
If we do not commit or show up,
We may lose the game
Or prolong it even more.
Outcomes may be different.
History may be different.
God is in control,
But we must be willing to move for His kingdom.

Be that warrior.
Be that leader.
Be a king or queen.
Do not fear,
For God will guide and provide.

Question your life.
The discovery of God's will is in front of you.
The key to unlocking yourself and others is in your hands.

Choose to play and defeat the enemy.

What is Hell?

Is hell a black pit where all fears are present?
Is hell full of the scariest of creatures?
Is hell in constant flames?

Or is hell a place where all our wants are located,
Allowing us to be chained without knowledge of being so?
Allowing us to never be content?
To never be full?
To never feel joy?

Maybe hell is different for everyone,
With a constant change of torture.

My Place in Heaven

The windows welcome light,
Feeding the greens,
Allowing color to blossom.

Sparkling light illuminates the paper on the
desk that sits patiently in the corner,
Awaiting daily conversation.
The ink is gold from the finest of earths
Ready to soak upon the finest sheets.

The French doors are open,
Allowing all inspiration the ability to be seen or heard.
The path is warmed by the glowing light,
Shadowed by the flowers that stand strong.

Every variety,
All with a meaning and healing purpose.
Planted in a maze with only the Creator
and keeper knowing the path.

At the center, a great tree sits with its branches full
And life flowing within.
Luminescent veins show a life's journey.
When touched, emotions are overwhelmed.
The body is uplifted,
And the most beautiful things are all present at once.

There sits a bench with water streaming nearby.
This is where we meet.
We talk.
We gather.
My forever home.

When the gates of heaven open,
Will you be there to walk through?

My Prayer

I pray that we learn from our past,
That we choose not to erase or ignore
But that we acknowledge and embrace
the beauty of overcoming.

I pray that we forgive those who have wronged
us, so we do not wrong others.

I pray that we decide to love ourselves no matter who we are,
What we've done,
Or the price tag associated with our names.

I pray that without war we find our friends
among our thought enemies.

I pray that we each find importance in our lives,
Importance in ourselves,
In the people around us,
And in the environment that supports us.

I pray that we listen, see, and touch the events around us,
That each past, present, and future memory resides within us.
Let it teach love, loss, and pain.
But above all, I pray that we are never alone
And that we can overcome any trouble
we may present ourselves with.

I pray that we take care of the little things
that may not have a voice—
Our children, other animals, the earth beneath our feet.

Let us follow our hearts, our minds, and never our habits.

God, I pray that our minds be renewed, our countries be renewed, and that all of humanity may be renewed.

I pray for this:
A new, embraced love and empowerment
for ourselves and everything.

What kind of world would you want a child to grow up in?

Lightning Source UK Ltd.
Milton Keynes UK
UKHW010621120919
349609UK00001B/308/P